YOUR KNOWLEDGE HAS V

Bibliographic information published by the German National Library:

The German National Library lists this publication in the National Bibliography; detailed bibliographic data are available on the Internet at http://dnb.dnb.de .

Imprint:

Copyright © 2018 GRIN Verlag
Print and binding: Books on Demand GmbH, Norderstedt Germany
ISBN: 9783668642607

This book at GRIN:

https://www.grin.com/document/413235

Mike Nkongolo

Demystifying Human Action Recognition in Deep Learning with Space-Time Feature Descriptors

GRIN Verlag

GRIN - Your knowledge has value

Since its foundation in 1998, GRIN has specialized in publishing academic texts by students, college teachers and other academics as e-book and printed book. The website www.grin.com is an ideal platform for presenting term papers, final papers, scientific essays, dissertations and specialist books.

Visit us on the internet:

http://www.grin.com/

http://www.facebook.com/grincom

http://www.twitter.com/grin_com

Demystifying Human Action Recognition in
Deep Learning with Space-Time Feature
Descriptors

Mike Nkongolo

February 16, 2018

Abstract

Human Action Recognition is the task of recognizing a set of actions being performed in a video sequence. Reliably and efficiently detecting and identifying actions in video could have vast impacts in the surveillance, security, healthcare and entertainment spaces. The problem addressed in this paper is to explore different engineered spatial and temporal image and video features (and combinations thereof) for the purposes of Human Action Recognition, as well as explore different Deep Learning architectures for non-engineered features (and classification) that may be used in tandem with the hand-crafted features. Further, comparisons between the different combinations of features will be made and the best, most discriminative feature set will be identified.

Contents

List of Figures

List of Tables

Chapter 1

Introduction

Human action recognition is a widely-studied area of research in computer vision and machine learning. This is most likely due to the fact that finding a possible, viable solution could have vast impacts in the surveillance, entertainment, and healthcare spaces (Ke et al., 2013). In the surveillance space, a solution would allow for detection of anomalous occurrences in surveillance footage, which could then trigger an alert to the relevant authorities/personnel. For instance, Facial Recognition is the new hot tech topic in China (see Figure 1.1).

Figure 1.1: A CCTV display using the facial-recognition system Face in Beijing (https://www.washingtonpost.com/news/world/wp/2018/01/07/).

Banks, airports, hotels and even public toilets are all trying to verify people's identities by analyzing their faces. Chinese's scientists used Facial Recognition and Artificial Intelligence to analyze and understand the mountain of incoming video evidence; to track suspects, spot suspicious behaviors and even predict crime; to coordinate the work of emergency services; and to monitor the comings and goings of the country's 1.4 billion people.

Further, automatic detection of unwanted events (e.g. shoplifting and fighting) would be possible. In the entertainment space, human-computer interaction would reach new levels of effectiveness since reliable detection of emotion and user behaviour would be possible. In the healthcare space, assistance in the rehabilitation of patients would be realisable.

However, finding such a generalised solution is still an open problem. This is most likely due to the fact that there are many common issues that plague video-based Human Action Recognition. For instance, occlusions in natural human appearance are rife, with problems such as differing clothing. This can dramatically effect the robustness and representational power of the extracted features. Additionally, there is the problem of perspective changes and viewpoint variation in the actual video sequences. This problem occurs because of camera angle changes and human pose changes. Most current solutions to Human Action Recognition are limited to a small set of possible viewpoints of the humans. Any datasets in which these perspective changes, occlusions, and complicated backgrounds are rife (e.g. Hollywood2) have very poor state-of-the-art performance.

The Human Action Recognition problem can be posed as attempting to estimate a mapping $f : \mathbb{R}^n \longrightarrow C$, where C is the finite set of action classes under consideration (*i.e.* $0 < |C| < \infty$), and n is the dimensionality of the feature vectors. The problem is typically divided into three main stages (Ke et al., 2013):

- Object segmentation

- Feature extraction and representation

- Classification

The object segmentation stage involves extracting key frames - frames in which actions of interest are occurring. These key frames can then be fed into the feature extraction phase, in which a robust, highly-discriminative set of features $\{p_i | p_i \in \mathbb{R}^n\}_i^M$ is extracted from each video sequence, where p_i

2

is the ith feature vector from the set of M feature vectors. The features can be extracted using any approach (e.g. gradient-based features), but typically should contain both spatial and temporal information. This set of features can then be combined and/or conglomerated in some novel fashion.

The feature extraction and representation phase involves extracting powerful features that can then be fed into some classification algorithm. These features must capture as much salient space-time information as possible, while disregarding as much unimportant information as possible. In other words, the features need to capture both pertinent motion and shape/appearance information in the video sequence. Typically, these features are computed by extracting local descriptors from some set of detected interest points, however, other techniques such as body modeling and frequency domain approaches also exist (Ke *et al.*, 2013). Once this novel set of feature descriptors has been computed, they can be used to train a classifier. Examples of function approximation and classification algorithms used to estimate f are Support Vector Machines and Neural Networks.

In this paper, we will investigate a method to solve the problem of Human Action Recognition. Chapter 2 will present a detailed, concise literature review of what relevant work has been done in this problem domain in the fields of Machine Learning and Computer Vision. The current state-of-the-art approach to the problem will also be identified and discussed in Chapter 2. Chapter 3 will discuss the proposed methodologies being employed in this paper, as well as the techniques that will be used. Chapter 4 will present a research plan and time line, including deliverables at each stage of development, as well as possible issues that could arise (and probable solutions to each). Lastly, Chapter 5 will give an overview of the proposed research, past research, along with emphasis on the obtained results.

Chapter 2

Background and Related Work

Human Action Recognition has been widely studied in the machine learning and Computer Vision research communities. It is a problem domain that could have great impact if solved in a generalised manner. There is still much work to be done in this area as most performance on non-trivial benchmark datasets is still relatively poor. The core of any Human Action Recognition problem is the feature extraction and representation. Without very reliable, highly-discriminative features, performance degrades very quickly. Additionally, such a set of features should contain only the pertinent and salient information in the video sequence (in both the spatial and temporal domain), while ignoring as much irrelevant information and noise as possible.

Most approaches adopt a hand-crafted feature engineering approach for the feature extraction phase (Laptev, 2005); (Schuldt et al., 2004); (Schuldt et al., 2004); (Wang et al., 2009); (Kienzle et al., 2007)-combining various features within the video sequence in a hierarchical manner. Often, a bag-of-features approach is then employed on this extracted feature set, and fed into a novel classification algorithm such as a Support Vector Machine or Neural Network. However, with the recent onset of Deep Learning in academia and industry, feature extraction approaches leveraging Deep Learning techniques are more frequently being utilised. This is often in the form of an automated feature learning process whereby the Deep Learning algorithm is tasked with learning a novel set of features from the raw data/pixels (Ravanbakhsh et al., 2015). Otherwise, Deep Learning techniques may be used in one or more steps of the hierarchical feature extraction process.

Such multi-faceted approaches are almost always employed, as they can be hand-engineered to accommodate for, and include, both the temporal and spatial information. Thus, these approaches often yield the best performance and results since they are able to distinguish between actions more reliably and robustly. Furthermore, one common intuition behind a hierarchical approach is the fact that most human actions consist of complex temporal compositions of more simple, base actions (Ravanbakhsh *et al.*, 2015). Either approach, however, can be effective if particular attention is given to the features fed into the models.

2.1 Feature Extraction and Descriptor Representation

Particular interest is given to the feature extraction stage of any video-based Human Action Recognition task, since extracting discriminative features is a formidable challenge. Most approaches employ an interest point detection mechanisms to localise points of interest in the video sequence, and then calculate some gradient, flow, or texture-based descriptor around those interest points. Following this, a bag-of-features (BoF) approach is typically taken in order to compute a fixed-length feature for the videos. Some approaches, however, instead opt for a feature learning approach, where the adopted machine learning model is set with the task of learning the appropriate features that can discriminate between the human actions.

2.1.1 Space-Time Interest Points (STIP)

The Harris interest point detector was extended into the temporal domain by Laptev (2005). The detector can localise spatio-temporal interest points in an image sequence. This interest point detection mechanism has been widely employed in the context of Human Action Recognition (Laptev, 2005); (Kovashka and Grauman, 2010). When used, it is typically considered the first stage in the feature engineering process to obtain the eventual full video features. They are computed by finding the local maxima (at a range of spatial and temporal scale values) of $H = det(\mu)\text{-}kTrace^3(\mu)$, where H is the interest point operator; μ is the spatio-temporal second-moment matrix; $k \in \mathbb{R}$ is a hyperparameter; $Trace$ is the trace operator for a matrix (Nkongolo, 2017); and det is the determinant operator for a matrix (Nkongolo and Kalonji, 2017); (Laptev and Lindeberg, 2006). The multi-scale approach is often taken as it is more computationally efficient than scale selection, as in regular Harris interest point detection. The core difference between the 2D Harris and 3D Harris algorithms is that convolution at the various stages occurs with 3D anisotropic separable Gaussian kernel with independent spatial and temporal variances, given by:

$$g(x, y, t; \sigma_l^2; \tau_l^2) = \frac{1}{\sqrt{(2\pi)^3 \sigma_l^4 \tau_l^2}} exp(-\frac{x^2 - y^2}{2\sigma_l^2} - \frac{t^2}{2\tau_l^2}) \qquad (2.1)$$

where x and y are spatial coordinates, and t is time; σ_l^2 and τ_l^2 are the independent spatial and temporal variances, respectively. Using this separate scale τ_l for the temporal domain is essential, since the spatial and temporal extents are, in general, independent (Ke et $al.$, 2013). Examples of detected STIPs can be seen in Figure 2.1.

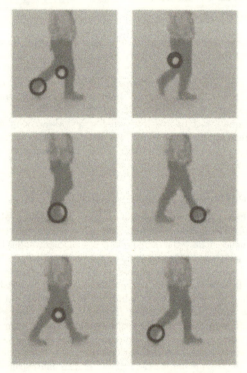

Figure 2.1: Example of Detected Space-Time Interest Points (Author's own work).

Schuldt et $al.$ (2004) implemented STIPs for the purposes of Human Action Recognition on the KTH dataset, which consists of six action classes:

walking; jogging; running; boxing; hand clapping; and hand waving. This was done by detecting points at combinations of pre-defined spatial and temporal scales. These two scales define the extent/neighbourhood of that interest point. Similarly, Klaser *et al.* (2008) implemented STIP as the sparse interest point detector that the eventual video features were based on, in order to classify human actions in three action recognition datasets. The detected STIPs were used as the basis for a new, novel spatio-temporal descriptor that is based on 3D gradients. Futher, Yuan *et al.* (2011) used STIPs as the starting point for developing features for action detection in video sequences. Lastly, Kovashka and Grauman (2010) used STIPs (as well as dense sampling) as the interest point detection step in developing discriminative hierarchical space-time features for the purposes of Human Action Recognition.

2.1.2   Dense Sampling

Dense sampling extracts interest points at regular positions and scales in space (and time for image sequences). Dense sampling is not often used in favour of STIPs, since they typically result in 15 to 20 times more interest points than the latter, which has a large effect on computational complexity and the ability to make a viable real-time system. Wang *et al.* (2009) evaluated dense sampling (among other techniques) as a method of extracting discriminative interest points in videos for the purposes of Human Action Recognition. Results showed that dense sampling outperforms other interest point detection methods in natural-scene video settings.

2.1.3   Histogram of Oriented Gradients (HOG)

HOG features were first used as image features in Dalal and Triggs (2005) for the purposes of human detection. Since then, HOG features have been used extensively for a wide variety of tasks. In the Human Action Recognition domain, HOG, or extensions of HOG (e.g. HOG3D), has been used extensively as a descriptor around detected interest points (Kovashka and Grauman, 2010); (Schuldt *et al.*, 2004).

HOG features are computed by breaking the image up into image patches, and for each of these image patches create a histogram of the gradient orientations, concatenated together. The final histogram is then normalized. This process is visualised by Figure 2.2 bellow.

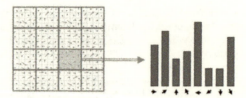

Figure 2.2: Example of HOG calculation (Author's own work).

Kovashka and Grauman (2010) used a three-dimensional extension of HOG features to create a novel spatiotemporal image descriptor. In it, 3D gradients are computed for a given image cube (i.e. a video sequence). In order to enable efficient computation of mean gradient vectors, the authors extended the integral image (popularised by Viola and Jones (2004) for use in Haar-wavelet-based face detection), to the concept of an integral video. The formula for the integral video is given by:

$$iv_{\partial z}(x, y, t) = \sum_{x' \leq x, y' \leq y, z' \leq z} v_{\partial z}(x', y', z') \tag{2.2}$$

where $z \in x, y, t$. The gradient orientations are then binned into a histogram and quantized. Klaser et al. (2008) employed HOG features as the appearance features for the purpose of efficient action detection in a video sequence. This is due to the fact that HOG features are adept at capturing the shape information of the object, for objects with clearly defined silhouettes and/or contours. Wang et al. (2009) evaluated numerous interest point detector and feature descriptor combinations, including HOG and its 3D extension - HOG3D, introduced by Kovashka and Grauman (2010)-for the purposes of Human Action Recognition. Similarly, Kovashka and Grauman (2010) also extract HOG and its 3D extension as features to build a hierarchy of discriminative space-time neighbourhood features for the same Human Action ecognition purpose.

2.1.4 N-Jets

Once interest points are found (whether from dense sampling, an interest point detector, or any other detection mechanism), descriptors known as N-Jets can computed around the interest points as a feature representation of the point. These N-jets are given by:

$$j = (L_x, L_y, L_t, L_{xx}, ..., L_t N)|_{\sigma^2 = \bar{\sigma}^2; \tau^2 = \bar{\tau}^2} \tag{2.3}$$

where $L_x^m y^n t^k = \sigma^m + n_\tau k(\frac{\partial}{\partial x^m \partial y^n \partial t^k} g * f)$; N is the maximum order of the partial derivatives; $\bar{\sigma}_i$ and $\bar{\tau}_i$ are the spatial and temporal scales at which that particular interest point was detected, respectively; f is the input image cube; and g is the three-dimensional Gaussian kernel. These descriptors, contrary to HOG, take into account temporal information.

Such descriptors have been utilised for the purposes of human action recognition, most notably by Ke et al. (2013). Ke et al. (2013) implemented third-order local jets as the feature descriptor choice for the detected spatiotemporal interest points. Similarly, Laptev and Lindeberg (2006) implemented fourth-order local jets as the descriptor choice of the detected space-time interest points that were found using the 3D extension of the Harris operator.

2.1.5 Histograms of Oriented Optical Flow (HOF)

Histograms of Oriented Optical Flow (along with HOG, and other gradient based feature descriptors) have been used extensively in the problem of action recognition, and more specifically, Human Action Recognition. In order for the HOF feature to be useful in an action recognition context, it needs to be scale invariant and invariant to the direction of motion. In order to compute the HOF feature vector, the optical flow at every frame of the video first needs to be computed. Each flow vector is then binned according to its primary angle from the horizontal and weighted according to its magnitude.

Formally, all optical flow vectors $v = [x, t]^T$ with direction $\theta = tan^{-1}(\frac{x}{y})$, in the range $-\frac{\pi}{2} + \pi\frac{b-1}{B} \leq \theta < -\frac{\pi}{2} + \pi\frac{b}{B}$, will contribute $\sqrt{x^2 + y^2}$ to the sum in bin b, $1 \leq b \leq B$, out of a total of B bins. The final histogram is then normalised to sum to 1. The normalisation step makes the HOF feature descriptor scale invariant. Lastly, in order to compare HOF features with each other, special care needs to be taking when choosing the appropriate kernel. A visualisation of these feature descriptors over time can be seen in Figure 2.3 bellow.

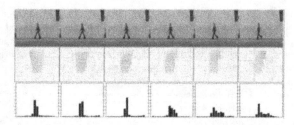

Figure 2.3: Visualisation of HOF features over time (Author's own work).

Chaudhry *et al.* (2009) implemented these features for the purposes of action recognition, positing that the natural feature to use in a motion sequence is optical flow-based. Yuan *et al.* (2011) used HOF as the extracted motion feature for the purposes of human action detection. Wang *et al.* (2009) included a combination of HOG and HOF features as one of the evaluated descriptors for the purpose of action recognition.

2.1.6 Feature Combination

Most approaches taken to create feature descriptors for the purposes of action recognition are multi-faceted or based on a bag-of-words/bag-or-features (BoW/BoF) approach. For instance, Klaser *et al.* (2008) used 3D HOG feature vectors as the base descriptor for a video sequence, where each video sequence contains a different number of these descriptors. These feature vectors were computed around detected STIPs. A BoW approach was then taken: For the whole training set of 3D HOG features (all descriptors from all videos), a subset of V features were sampled. These V samples were then clustered using k-means. This builds a so-called vocabulary of visual words. The final feature descriptor for a given video sequence is then given by a histogram of visual word occurrences for each 3D HOG vector from that sequence (i.e. closest visual word from the k-means result to the current feature vector, based on Euclidean distance).

A somewhat similar approach was taken by Laptev (2005) in which a BoF technique was employed, where the feature vectors were third-order local jets computed around STIPs. A subset of all the jets from the training set were then sampled, and clustered using k-means to produce a vocabulary of visual words. As in Klaser *et al.* (2008), the final feature vector was a histogram of visual word occurrences for each jet feature from the given video sequence. The distance metric used, however, was Mahalanobis distance:

10

$d^2(j_1, j_2) = (j_1 - j_2) \sum^{-1} (j_1 - j_2)^T$; where $\sum^{-1}$ is the inverse of the covariance matrix of the data; and $j_1, j_2 \in \mathbb{R}^n$ are two vectors. Schuldt *et al.* (2004) took a similar feature extraction approach to this, where the only difference is that the local jet features were fourth-order as opposed to third-order as in Klaser *et al.* (2008).

Laptev *et al.* (2008) extracted STIPs at various predefined spatial and temporal scales, as opposed to conventional scale selection (since this is more computationally efficient). Features that characterise motion and appearance of these local interest points (at the relevant scales) were then extracted: HOG (appearance) and HOF (motion). This HOG/HOF feature is similar in nature to the well-known SIFT descriptor. The descriptor was then a normalised histogram of the concatenated HOG and HOF feature vectors. A BoF approach was then employed by k-means clustering, a subset of the training HOG/HOF descriptors, and once again computing a histogram of visual word occurrences (closest vocabulary word to the current feature based on Euclidean distance).

Lastly, a completely different approach was taken by Ravanbakhsh *et al.* (2015). They employed a hierarchical feature extraction model. First, for spatial features, the output of the fc7 layer[1] in an ImageNet-trained AlexNet convolutional neural network (CNN) was used. Then, in order to capture the temporal variation in the image sequences, a hierarchical model based on the intuition that complex actions are made up simple base actions, was used. So-called CNN-flows were computed. In order to do this, M key frames (frames where it is likely that actions are taking place) need to be selected. Once selected, these key frames are mapped to the CNN feature space. The CNN flows (analogous to the Lucas-Kanade optical flow method) are then computed by subtracting the last CNN key frame from the first CNN key frame in the current sequence. The sequence is then partitioned in a binary tree fashion, and the process is repeated two more times on the resulting nodes. PCA[2] is applied to each successive layer of this tree structure in order to reduce computational cost by reducing the dimensionality of the data. A BoW approach is then taken by clustering the data using k-means (as with the above-described approaches), and histograms of visual word occurrences are computed as the final video sequence features, where the features used in the histogram computation are the CNN flows from each layer of the binary tree.

---

[1] Last Convolutional Layer.
[2] Principal Component Analysis

In a similar Deep Learning approach to Ravanbakhsh *et al.* (2015), Baccouche *et al.* (2011) left it up to the machine learning model (a convolutional and recurrent neural network hybrid) to learn the features from raw pixel values (i.e. from the actual training videos). The intuition was that the neural network would learn the salient and latent features during training, and there would be no need for manual, hand-crafted feature engineering as with all other approaches.

2.2 Learning Algorithms

Learning algorithms, though important, only come second to feature extraction in terms of importance in Human Action Recognition problems. The most common approach to take is to use the state-of-the-art classifier at the time of research, which in the case of this problem domain are support vector machines and deep neural network architectures such as convolutional and recurrent nets.

2.2.1 Support Vector Machines (SVM)

Support Vector Machines are the state-of-the-art large margin classifiers, and have been utilised for the purpose of Human Action Recognition by Schuldt *et al.* (2004). The SVM optimization problem can be formulated as follows. Given a binary classification problem with training set $\{x_i, y_i\}_M^i$, $x_i \in \mathbb{R}$, $y_i \in \{-1, 1\}$ where x_i and y_i are the ith feature vectors and target values, respectively, and M is the number of these predictor-response pairs in the set, the problem is optimally separate the two classes. Assume the two classes can be separated by the hyperplane $w^T x + b = 0$ in some space $\mathbb{H}$ (w and b are parameters), and that we have no prior knowledge about the distribution of the data. The optimal hyperplane is then the one which maximizes the margin (distance between the two classes). Optimal values for b and w can be found by solving the following constrained minimization problem using Lagrange multipliers α_i :

$$f(x) = \mathbf{sign}(\sum_{i=1}^{m} \alpha_i y_i K(x_i, x) + b) \tag{2.4}$$

where K is a kernel function - commonly a linear or radial basis function; y_i is the ith target value of the dataset; x_i is the ith feature vector from the data; m is the number of samples in the dataset, and **sign** is defined as:

12

$$\mathbf{sign}(x) = \begin{cases} -1 & \text{if } x < 0, \\ 0 & \text{if } x = 0, \\ 1 & \text{if } x > 0. \end{cases} \tag{2.5}$$

In the context of Human Action Recognition, the χ^2 kernel is often adopted due to its suitably for the features extracted from the video sequences. This kernel is given by $K(S_i, S_j) = exp(-\frac{1}{2A}\sum_{n=1}^{V}(\frac{(s_{in}-s_{ij})^2}{s_{in}+s_{jn}}))$ where V is the vocabulary size, and A is the mean of the distances between all training samples. Schuldt et al. (2004) implemented a linear SVM with the above-mentioned histogram of visual word occurrences based on clustered fourth-order spatio-temporal jets as features. This combination results in an average accuracy of 71% across the six action classes of the KTH dataset. Klaser et al. (2008) implemented a non-linear SVM with the χ^2 kernel for testing their new, novel 3D gradient-based spatio-temporal descriptor (3DHOG) on three different human action recognition datasets - KTH; Weizmann; and Hollywood. The achieved average class accuracies for the three datasets were 91.4%, 84.3%, and 24.7%, respectively (with the aforementioned BoF approach).

Wang et al. (2009) evaluated the performance of various combinations of interest point detectors and feature descriptors in the context of Human Action Recognition on three different datasets - KTH, UCF, and Hollywood2. In all scenarios, a bag of features approach was taken in which the extracted spatio-temporal features were clustered using k-means clustering to form a key vocabulary of visual words. Representations for the videos are then given by histograms of visual word occurrences. For the classification, a non-linear SVM with the χ^2 kernel was used. The interest point detectors that were considered were: (1) Harris3D; (2) Cuboids; (3) Hessian; (4) Dense. The descriptors that were evaluated were: (1) HOG3D; (2) HOG/HOF; (3) HOG; (4) HOF; (5) Cuboids; (6) ESURF.

The findings were by Wang et al. (2009) were that simple dense sampling consistently outperforms the interest point detectors in realistic video settings. However, dense sampling's increased computational complexity due to number of interest points detected needs to be taken into consideration. Further, the detectors all perform similarly on the studied datasets. With respect to descriptors, gradient-based and optical-flow based descriptors provide consistently good results. Tables 2.1 and 2.2 show some of the results from the paper.

13

Table 2.1: Average accuracy for various detector/descriptor combinations on the KTH dataset (Wang et al., 2009).

	HOG3D	HOG/HOF	HOG	HOG	Cuboids	ESURF
Harris3D	89.0%	91.8%	80.9%	92.1%	-	-
Cuboids	90.0%	88.7%	82.3%	88.2%	89.1%	-
Hessian	84.6%	88.7%	77.7%	88.6%	-	81.4%
Dense	85.3%	86.1%	79.0%	88.0%	-	-

Table 2.2: Average accuracy for various detector/descriptor combinations on the UCF dataset (Wang et al., 2009).

	HOG3D	HOG/HOF	HOG	HOG	Cuboids	ESURF
Harris3D	79.7%	78.1%	71.4%	75.4%	-	-
Cuboids	82.9%	77.7%	72.7%	76.7%	76.6%	-
Hessian	79.0%	79.3%	66.0%	75.3%	-	77.3%
Dense	85.6%	81.6%	77.4%	82.6%	-	-

2.2.2 Convolutional Neural Networks (CNN)

A convolutional neural network is a - commonly deep - neural architecture used for processing data that has a known grid-like topology (Goodfellow et al., 2016). For this reason, it is widely used for image recognition and classification tasks. At a basic level, CNNs can be thought of as regular neural networks that use convolution in place of general matrix multiplication in at least one of their layers. Due to the current accessibility and commonality of fast computational devices, there has been a wide adoption of Deep Learning models such as CNNs. Moreover, CNNs have become the state-of-the-art technique in many computer vision tasks, with the famous ImageNet challenge being dominated by CNNs and similar deep architectures.

In CNNs, it is common to have multiple sequential convolutional and max pooling layers, followed by an eventually fully-connected layer that performs the classification step. The pooling layers provide approximate location invariance to the system. Furthermore, there is typically a non-linearity introduced on to the output of the convolutional layer (before the pooling layer) in the form of a non-linear activation function. This activation function can be any function that is: 1) Non-constant; 2) Bounded; 3) Monotonically increasing; and 4) Continuous. In CNNs, it is usually the rectified linear unit (ReLU) activation function $f(x) = max(x, 0)$, since the usual sigmoid activation $g(x) = \frac{1}{1+e^{-x}}$ exacerbates the vanishing gradient problem. These conditions for the activation functions are necessary in order for the universal approximation theorem (any function of N variables defined on a compact subset of $\mathbb{R}^N$ can be approximated by a three-layer neural network with such an activation function) to hold. Lastly, a concept known as dropout is often employed in CNNs, whereby during training a certain portion of the neurons in any particular layer are 'turned off'. This is done to combat over-fitting.

Ravanbakhsh et al. (2015) used an SVM trained on the previously-described BoF hierarchical CNN and CNN-flow features for the purpose of human action recognition on the KTH, UCF-11, and UCF Sport datasets. This is an example of combining hand-crafted feature with Deep Learning models. The approach resulted in average accuracies for the three datasets of 95.6%, 97.8%, and 89.5%, respectively. This is close to state-of-the-art performance for the three datasets. In a similar Deep Learning vain, Baccouche et al. (2011) implemented a hybrid convolution neural network and recurrent neural network approach to the Human Action Recognition problem. It was left up to this neural network to learn the salient features that would discriminate between the action classes in the studied dataset (KTH). This is an example of feature learning since the algorithm must learn features from raw pixels values (from the training videos). The architecture of the hybrid neural network was 7 3D convolution and pooling/sub-sampling layers, followed by a fully-connected recurrent layer, and finally, the output softmax layer, which would make the predictions. The activation function for the convolutional layers was the ReLu function $f(x) = max(x, 0)$, and the units in the recurrent layers were Long Short-Term Memory (LSTM) units.

2.2.3 Recurrent Neural Networks (RNNs)

RNNs are a family of neural networks for processing sequential data (Goodfellow et al., 2016). That is, whereas a CNN is particularly well-suited for processing grid-like data, an RNN is well-suited for processing inherently sequential data such as time-series data, or videos. In RNNs, some of the connections are feedback connections, which enables the network (given the right neuron type - LSTM or GRU) to have some form of memory - which is essential when modelling sequences. This allows the networks to learn local and long-term dependencies in the data, as well as take variable-length input. Because of these feedback connections, the activity of any given neuron in the RNN is dependent upon both the output of the previous layer, as well as the output of the current neuron at the previous time step.

Mathematically:

$$a^{(t)} = b + Wh^{(t-1)} + Ux^{(t)} \qquad (2.6)$$

$$h^{(t)} = \gamma(a^{(t)}) \qquad (2.7)$$

$$o^{(t)} = c + Vh^{(t)} \qquad (2.8)$$

$$\widehat{y}^{(t)} = \mathbf{softmax}(o^{(t)}) \qquad (2.9)$$

where t is the time step; x is the input; y is the target; U, V, and W are the input-to-hidden, hidden-to-output, and hidden-to-hidden weight matrices, respectively; b and c are bias vectors; γ is an activation function; h is the hidden representation of the input, a is the activity of the neuron, and o is the output, which once sent through the softmax function (resulting in $\widehat{y}$), is compared to the real target value (Goodfellow *et al.*, 2016).

Baccouche *et al.* (2011) implemented a hybrid neural network where an RNN with LSTM units was employed after the convolutional layers. The intuition behind this is that since Human Action Recognition is partially a sequential/time-series problem (each frame of an action depends on the previous frame/s). The CNN part of the network would model and extract the pertinent features of the videos, and the RNN would accurately model how these features interact/relate and classify into one of the action classes accordingly. This hybrid approach resulted in an average accuracy of 94.39% across the six action classes of the KTH dataset, which is close to state-of-the-art performance for the dataset.

2.3   Conclusion

As can be seen from this survey, many different approaches have been taken to solve the Human Action Recognition problem. Further, the majority of the research focus in this area is indeed in the feature engineering and extraction. Most approaches tend to adopt a hierarchical feature extraction process, whereby many features are combined and conglomerated to form a final set of highly-discriminative features. These features are often gradient-based, such as HOG, HOF, and N-Jets. However, these may be any features, such as those extracted from a forward pass in a pre-trained CNN.

State-of-the-art approaches employ hand-crafted feature engineering, along with hierarchical and/or BoF techniques to find a novel set of features that can be fed into a classifier. These classifiers are often SVMs or neural network models.

However, there is definitely still a need for a robust, real-time solution to the problem. Hand-crafted (hierarchical) features do indeed perform well, but in specific scenarios (for certain datasets). The extracted features do not typically generalise well between datasets. This problem, however, may be solved using Deep Learning techniques, since CNNs and other deep neural architectures have achieved state-of-the-art performance in many computer vision tasks (e.g. image recognition, object detection, etc.). That is, a somewhat generalized solution to Human Action Recognition could be achieved using automated feature learning with Deep Learning techniques.

Chapter 3

Research Method

In the previous section, the multitude of approaches and techniques that have been chosen to solve the problem of Human Action Recognition were reviewed. The best approaches typically pay careful attention to the features that are fed into the Machine Learning models, and particularly, how these features are engineered. This chapter serves to clearly detail the objectives of the research, and the research methodology that will be followed during the course of the research.

3.1 Research Hypothesis

Combining carefully-extracted gradient-based and/or Deep Learning-based features along with using an inherently-sequential model, a recurrent neural network, will allow for accurate and robust Human Action Recognition.

3.2 Methodology

3.2.1 Phase 1: Implementation

This initial phase is perhaps the longest in terms of time. It focuses mainly on the implementation of the described system to create the final robust and accurate Human Action Recognition system. These are the main tasks to complete in this phase:

- `Dataset collection`: This involves collecting the required Human Action Recognition datasets that will be used in the research. These datasets must consist of videos and multiple action classes.

- **Feature engineering:** This task includes designing and extracting a novel, discriminative set of features from the input videos from the datasets. This is probably the most important step in the research, as this step will partially directly effect the eventual recognition rates of the system. These features will be gradient-based spatio-temporal features, as well as Deep Learning-based features.

- **Classifier selection, design, and implementation:** This task is selecting, designing, and implementing an appropriate classifier for the system. This classifier will be trained on the features extracted.[1] The chosen classifier will be a recurrent neural network.

3.2.2 Phase 2: Training

At this phase of development of the system, the chosen classifier from the Implementation phase must be trained on the extracted features. This may be time-consuming since the model is a Deep model, and other factors such as architecture of network, feature design, computing power, etc. also may affect training time.

3.2.3 Phase 3: Testing

The whole system must be tested to see what detection rates result. A hold-out subset of the input dataset will be reserved for this purpose. Testing involves feeding test videos into the system, computing, and analysing the various metrics for performance (average accuracy and confusion matrices).

3.3 Motivation for Method

3.3.1 Features

The reason gradient-based spatio-temporal, and Deep Learning-based, features will be used is because of their great success at many different tasks in image recognition and object detection, and more importantly, human action recognition. Whether it is SIFT, HOG, HOF, or N-Jets, all of them are gradient-based and all have been used successfully in the action recognition domain. Further, the reason the features will be spatio-temporal (as opposed to just spatial) is due to the fact that in order to accurately and robustly recognise actions in video, the temporal information inherent in the

---

[1]From the Feature engineering step.

19

video must be taken into account. Without this, much information is being thrown away.

3.3.2 Classifier

The reason a recurrent neural network will be used is because it works best with sequential data, and videos are inherently sequential in nature. The current frame depends on, and is correlated with, the previous frames.

3.4 Conclusion

This chapter discussed the methodology that will be adopted for the proposed research. The first phase will involve designing and implementing the system using Python and the relevant libraries. This includes dataset collection; extraction of chosen features from that data; and finally features fed into the chosen Machine Learning model to train. Testing will then take place, and depending on the results, an iterative process will take place.

Chapter 4

Research Plan

In the previous chapter, the hypotheses for the paper, as well as the research methodologies to be employed, were introduced. However, this chapter serves to present the manner in which these aforementioned methodologies will be carried out in a formalized fashion.

This will include a detailed account of the tasks required at each stage, outlining the deliverables, a time schedule for these tasks, and finally, potential issues that may arise that could possibly hinder research progression (along with possible counteractions to them).

4.1 Deliverables

4.1.1 Phase 1: Implementation

- Dataset collection: Collect widely-studied Human Action Recognition benchmark datasets from the Internet. This includes the KTH and UCF datasets.

- Feature engineering: Design and implement gradient-based spatio-temporal features, as well as Deep Learning-based features, that capture both as much spatial and temporal information as possible. This step will also include any pre- and post-processing that may be required to be performed on the input video sequences.

- Classifier selection, design, and implementation: Design and implement the recurrent neural network classifier in the chosen architecture.

4.1.2 Phase 2: Training

Train the classifier as designed and implemented in the previous stage. The network will be trained on the features extracted from the input videos in the Feature Engineering phase. Additionally, this step will involve finding the optimal hyper-parameter settings and network architecture.

4.1.3 Phase 3: Testing

The trained classifier will be tested on a hold-out test set that is a subset of the original input videos collected in Phase 1. This will allow the various metrics for performance to be calculated.[1]

---

[1] Confusion matrix, and average accuracy.

Table 4.1: Time Plan for Research.

Week	Task
14-Aug-18	Dataset collection
21-Aug-18	Feature Engineering
28-Aug-18	Feature Engineering
04-Sep-18	Feature Engineering
11-Sep-18	Feature Engineering
18-Sep-18	Feature Engineering
25-Sep-18	Feature Engineering
02-Oct-18	Feature Engineering
09-Oct-18	Classifier implementation
16-Oct-18	Classifier implementation
23-Oct-18	Training system
30-Oct-18	Training system
30-Oct-18	Training system
06-Nov-18	Training system
06-Nov-18	Testing
13-Nov-18	Testing
04-Dec-18	System deployment

The time plan for the creation and implementation of the whole system with respect to the aforementioned phases of development is given in Table 4.1.

4.2 Potential Issues

4.2.1 Lengthy Training Time

The training phase may take an inordinate amount of time considering the fact that there are so many factors that affect it. The features could be too high dimensional; the neural network might contain too many trainable parameters; or the computing power might be too low. Consequently, should the training time prove to be too lengthy, a potential solution could be reducing the dimensionality of the features, changing the architecture of the network to reduce the number of trainable parameters, or move the training to a cluster to increase computing power significantly.

4.2.2 Low Accuracies

The problem of low recognition rates, and thus low accuracies, could be the result of many problems. Such problems could include ineffectual (unlearnable) features, not enough/too many training epochs, or difficulty of the problem at hand. Should the first problem occur, this could be mitigated by attempting to extract different, more discriminative features from the videos/data. If the problem is not enough or too many training epochs, this is easy enough to diagnose and solve.

4.3 Conclusion

As can be seen, this project requires that careful attention be taken at each stage of the research to ensure that the proposed time plan can be followed correctly and realistically. The time plan must be, and is, strict enough to allow for completion of the task, but flexible enough to allow one to overcome any unforeseen circumstances. Realistic time bounds (i.e. long enough to complete and short enough to complete the research in the allowed time) were proposed, and any likely issues that may arise during the research were identified, along with probable solutions to mitigate each.

Chapter 5

Conclusion

In this paper, the development and implementation of a robust framework for Human Action Recognition was proposed. The motivation behind the proposed research is, firstly, the high effectiveness of gradient-based features as descriptors - such as HOG, HOF, and N-Jets - for video-based human action recognition. They are capable of capturing both the salient spatial and temporal information in the video sequences, while removing much of the redundant information that is not pertinent to the action. Combining these features in a hierarchical fashion further increases performance.

Secondly, the motivation behind using an RNN is that it is made specifically to process time-series and/or sequential data. Videos are indeed sequential by nature, as every frame is dependent on the frames that came before it. Combining the above-described novel features with such a model will surely yield results comparative to that of the state-of-the-art. The intuition behind the choice of an RNN over the other popular inherently-sequential model, a Hidden Markov Model (HMM), is the fact that RNNs have surpassed HMMs as the state-of the-art in novel sequential data processing tasks such language translation and voice recognition.

The performance of the full system will be evaluated in the following manner. Certain metrics for performance will be computed such as confusion matrices and average accuracies. These performance metrics will then be compared to the same metrics achieved by other scientists with their methods for the same set of benchmark datasets. The feasibility of the proposed approach will be determined based on its performance thereof.

References

[Baccouche *et al.* 2011] Moez Baccouche, Franck Mamalet, Christian Wolf, Christophe Garcia, and Atilla Baskurt. Sequential deep learning for human action recognition. In *International Workshop on Human Behavior Understanding*, pages 29–39. Springer, 2011.

[Chaudhry *et al.* 2009] Rizwan Chaudhry, Avinash Ravichandran, Gregory Hager, and René Vidal. Histograms of oriented optical flow and binet-cauchy kernels on nonlinear dynamical systems for the recognition of human actions. In *computer vision and pattern recognition, 2009. CVPR 2009. IEEE Conference on*, pages 1932–1939. IEEE, 2009.

[Dalal and Triggs 2005] Navneet Dalal and Bill Triggs. Histograms of oriented gradients for human detection. In *Computer Vision and Pattern Recognition, 2005. CVPR 2005. IEEE Computer Society Conference on*, volume 1, pages 886–893. IEEE, 2005.

[Goodfellow *et al.* 2016] Ian Goodfellow, Yoshua Bengio, and Aaron Courville. Deep learning.(2016). *Book in preparation for MIT Press. URL: http://www. deeplearningbook. org*, 2016.

[Ke *et al.* 2013] Shian-Ru Ke, Hoang Le Uyen Thuc, Yong-Jin Lee, Jenq-Neng Hwang, Jang-Hee Yoo, and Kyoung-Ho Choi. A review on video-based human activity recognition. *Computers*, 2(2):88–131, 2013.

[Kienzle *et al.* 2007] Wolf Kienzle, Bernhard Schölkopf, Felix A Wichmann, and Matthias O Franz. How to find interesting locations in video: a spatiotemporal interest point detector learned from human eye movements. In *Joint Pattern Recognition Symposium*, pages 405–414. Springer, 2007.

[Klaser *et al.* 2008] Alexander Klaser, Marcin Marszalek, and Cordelia Schmid. A spatio-temporal descriptor based on 3d-gradients. In *BMVC 2008-19th British Machine Vision Conference*, pages 275–1. British Machine Vision Association, 2008.

[Kovashka and Grauman 2010] Adriana Kovashka and Kristen Grauman. Learning a hierarchy of discriminative space-time neighborhood features for human action recognition. In *Computer Vision and Pattern Recognition (CVPR), 2010 IEEE Conference on*, pages 2046–2053. IEEE, 2010.

[Laptev and Lindeberg 2006] Ivan Laptev and Tony Lindeberg. Local descriptors for spatio-temporal recognition. In *Spatial Coherence for Visual Motion Analysis*, pages 91–103. Springer, 2006.

[Laptev *et al.* 2008] Ivan Laptev, Marcin Marszalek, Cordelia Schmid, and Benjamin Rozenfeld. Learning realistic human actions from movies. In *Computer Vision and Pattern Recognition, 2008. CVPR 2008. IEEE Conference on*, pages 1–8. IEEE, 2008.

[Laptev 2005] Ivan Laptev. On space-time interest points. *International journal of computer vision*, 64(2-3):107–123, 2005.

[Nkongolo and Kalonji 2017] Mike Nkongolo and Roland Kalonji. Using cnc for mercedes benz logo design. 2017.

[Nkongolo 2017] Mike Nkongolo. A web-based prototype course recommender system using apache mahout. 2017.

[Ravanbakhsh *et al.* 2015] Mahdyar Ravanbakhsh, Hossein Mousavi, Mohammad Rastegari, Vittorio Murino, and Larry S Davis. Action recognition with image based cnn features. *arXiv preprint arXiv:1512.03980*, 2015.

[Schuldt *et al.* 2004] Christian Schuldt, Ivan Laptev, and Barbara Caputo. Recognizing human actions: a local svm approach. In *Pattern Recognition, 2004. ICPR 2004. Proceedings of the 17th International Conference on*, volume 3, pages 32–36. IEEE, 2004.

[Viola and Jones 2004] Paul Viola and Michael J Jones. Robust real-time face detection. *International journal of computer vision*, 57(2):137–154, 2004.

[Wang *et al.* 2009] Heng Wang, Muhammad Muneeb Ullah, Alexander Klaser, Ivan Laptev, and Cordelia Schmid. Evaluation of local spatio-temporal features for action recognition. In *BMVC 2009-British Machine Vision Conference*, pages 124–1. BMVA Press, 2009.

[Yuan *et al.* 2011] Junsong Yuan, Zicheng Liu, and Ying Wu. Discriminative video pattern search for efficient action detection. *IEEE Transactions on Pattern Analysis and Machine Intelligence*, 33(9):1728–1743, 2011.